DK SUPER History

# LEWIS AND CLARK EXPEDITION

Follow this historic expedition and meet all the people who made it possible, including Sacagawea

**PRODUCED FOR DK BY**
**Editorial** Just Content Limited
**Design** Studio Noel

**Author** Jennifer Kaul

**Senior Editor** Ankita Awasthi Tröger
**Editor** Hattie Hansford
**Senior Art Editor** Gilda Pacitti
**Graphic Story Illustrator** Matt Garbutt
**Managing Editor** Carine Tracanelli
**Managing Art Editor** Sarah Corcoran
**Pre-Production Coordinator** Shanker Prasad
**Pre-Production Designer** Jaypal Chauhan
**Production Controller** Rebecca Parton
**Publisher** Sarah Forbes
**Managing Director, Learning** Hilary Fine

First published in Great Britain in 2025 by
Dorling Kindersley Limited
20 Vauxhall Bridge Road,
London SW1V 2SA

The authorised representative in the EEA is
Dorling Kindersley Verlag GmbH. Arnulfstr. 124,
80636 Munich, Germany


10 9 8 7 6 5 4 3 2 1
001–350114–Sep/2025



A CIP catalogue record for this book
is available from the British Library.
ISBN: 978-0-2417-4473-4

Printed and bound in China

**www.dk.com**

This book was made with Forest Stewardship Council™ certified paper – one small step in DK's commitment to a sustainable future.
**Learn more at www.dk.com/uk/information/sustainability**

# Contents


History in Perspective 4

Key Events: What Happened When 6

Key People: Who's Who 8

Key Locations: Expedition Map 10

A Land of Many Cultures 12

Why Was There an Expedition? 14

Getting Ready 16

Heading West 18

Fort Mandan 20

From Mandan to the Pacific 22

Finally Reunited 24

A Challenging Winter 28

Returning Home 30

Westward Expansion 32

Indigenous People's Perspectives 34

Lessons from History 36

Uncovering the Truth: Primary Sources 38

Uncovering the Truth: Secondary Sources 40

Vocabulary Builder: Exploring the Land 42

Glossary 44

Index 46


Words in **bold** are explained in the glossary on page 44.

# History in Perspective

In 1804, Meriwether Lewis and William Clark set off on a **historic expedition**. They wanted to learn about the vast area of land west of the Mississippi River. This was land that the US **government** wanted to claim. Lewis and Clark's journey had a huge impact on them and their crew. It made them both famous. It also affected the future of the United States and the **Indigenous** peoples who already lived on the land.

## Where and when?

Lewis and Clark set off from St Louis, Missouri, on 14 May 1804. They travelled west to Oregon before heading back to Missouri. They returned to St Louis on 23 September 1806.

## Who was involved?

Lewis and Clark were the leaders of the expedition group. The group was called the Corps of Discovery. They hoped to discover new plants and animals and meet with Indigenous communities. They wanted to find a **waterway** to the Pacific Ocean to expand **trade**. Finally, they planned to record their journey by drawing maps and writing journal entries.

Indigenous peoples had been living on the land west of the Mississippi River for thousands of years. Many were welcoming to guests. Others were **wary** of them. These different reactions likely came from each group's past experiences, their **culture** and their wants and needs at the time.

Interactions between Indigenous peoples and the crew of the Corps of Discovery were not always positive. This painting shows the group meeting an Indigenous community of the Pacific Northwest.

# Different perspectives

Different groups in society may have deeply contrasting experiences of events. Official records of the past often only present one side of the story. This means that they can't reflect the experiences of everyone affected. To understand what happened, it is important that we look at events from more than one point of view.

## Think about it

What kinds of **sources** could we use to learn about the expedition?

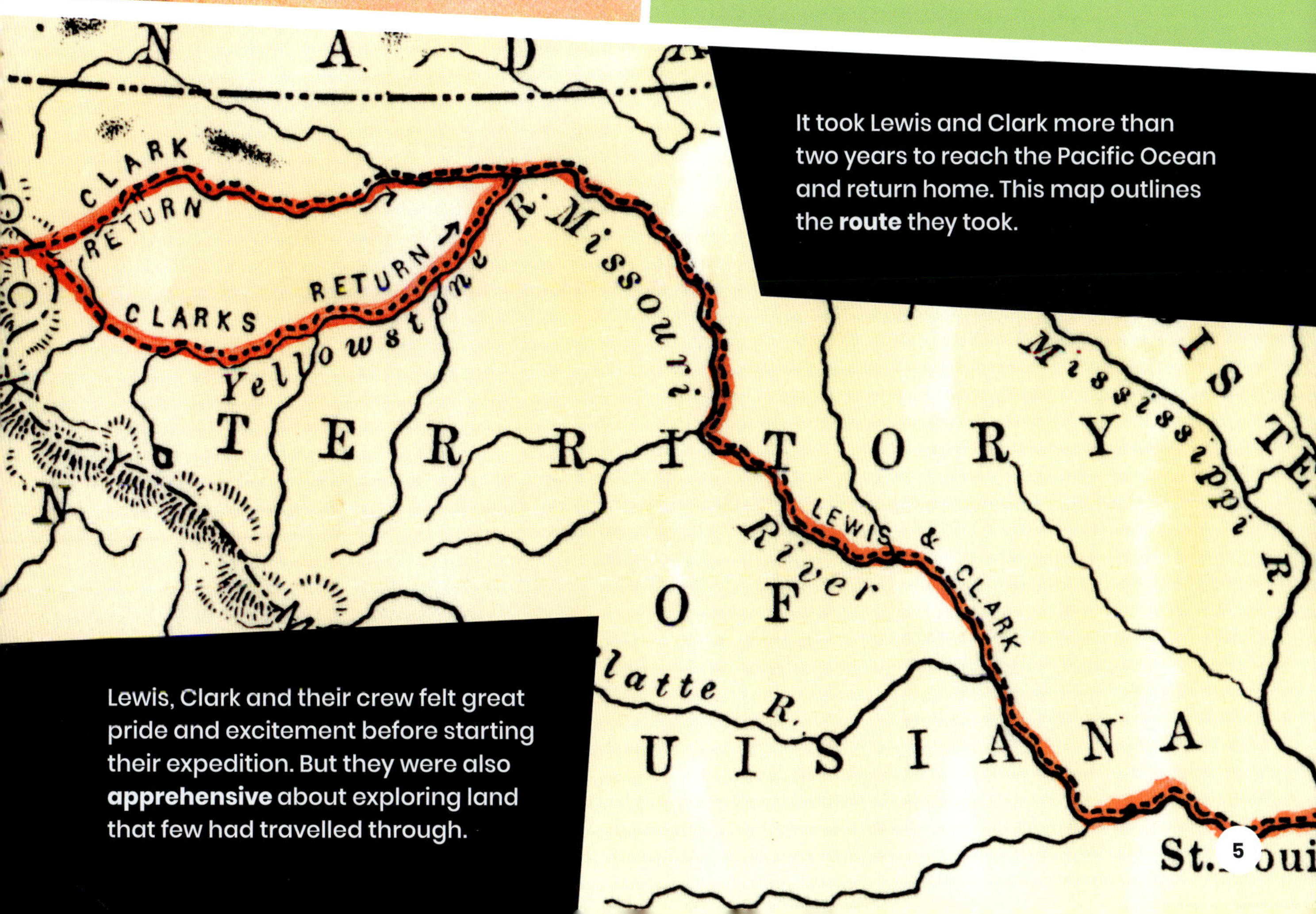


It took Lewis and Clark more than two years to reach the Pacific Ocean and return home. This map outlines the **route** they took.

Lewis, Clark and their crew felt great pride and excitement before starting their expedition. But they were also **apprehensive** about exploring land that few had travelled through.

# Key Events
# WHAT HAPPENED WHEN

The expedition changed the United States forever. Lewis and Clark explored land that had never been officially documented. They met many Indigenous communities along the way and found several new **species** of wildlife.

## 1803

**2 MAY**

France sells a large area of land to the US. This is known as the Louisiana Purchase. Indigenous communities already live there – the land has been their home for thousands of years.

**4 JULY**

President Jefferson tells the American people about the Louisiana Purchase. He announces a planned expedition to explore the land.

## 1804

**14 MAY**

The expedition sets off from Camp Dubois near St Louis, Missouri.

### 2 NOVEMBER

The crew starts building Fort Mandan so they have somewhere to stay over the winter. Toussaint Charbonneau and his wife, Sacagawea, join them there.

### 7 NOVEMBER

The crew gets their first glimpse of the Pacific Ocean.

### 24 NOVEMBER

The crew votes on where to stay for the winter. The vote includes York, a Black man **enslaved** by Clark. Sacagawea also shares her opinion, but her vote is not counted.

## 1805

### 7 APRIL

A small group leaves the expedition. They return home with maps, letters, plant and animal **specimens**, and more to share with President Jefferson.

## 1806

### 23 SEPTEMBER

The expedition returns home. The US government celebrates and rewards the crew for their achievements.

# Key People
# WHO'S WHO

The Lewis and Clark expedition affected many people. It impacted the individuals involved in the journey and those living on the land they travelled through. Many **interpreters**, mapmakers and other crew members were important for its success. Here are some of the key figures in this story.

Thomas Jefferson

## The organiser

### Thomas Jefferson

The third president of the United States. He was also one of the authors of the **Declaration of Independence**.

William Clark

## The leaders

### Meriwether Lewis

A military **captain**. He was chosen by President Jefferson to lead the expedition.

### William Clark

A **lieutenant** and friend of Lewis. Lewis asked him to help lead the expedition.

# The crew

**York**
An enslaved man forced to join Clark on the journey. His first name is unknown.

**Toussaint Charbonneau**
A French-Canadian fur trader. He made a deal with the Hidatsa people to buy Sacagawea as his wife.

**Sacagawea**
An Indigenous woman of the Shoshone people. She was captured by the Hidatsa people when she was 12 years old. She and her husband acted as interpreters for the rest of the crew.

**Jean Baptiste Charbonneau**
The son of Charbonneau and Sacagawea. He was born on the expedition and was later raised by Clark.

**John Ordway**
A military **sergeant** who distributed supplies and kept records for the expedition. He also kept a journal about their interactions with Indigenous peoples.

**Patrick Gass**
An army ranger, **carpenter** and boat builder. He also kept a journal of the expedition, and made many engravings.

**Charles Floyd**
A military sergeant. He was the only crew member who died on the expedition.

**Seaman**
A Newfoundland dog that Lewis purchased to join the crew on the expedition.

Patrick Gass

York
Seaman

# Key Locations
# EXPEDITION MAP

Fort Clatsop

Columbia River

Lewis and Clark were sent to explore land that had recently been purchased by the United States. President Jefferson hoped they would learn more about the land, its people and its **resources** during their expedition. He also hoped they would find a waterway that would lead to the Pacific Ocean.

The expedition set off from St Louis in May 1804, travelling west. They made many stops along the way, finally reaching the Pacific Ocean in November 1805. The group split up on the way back, but came back together for the final part of the journey. The entire trip took nearly two and a half years.

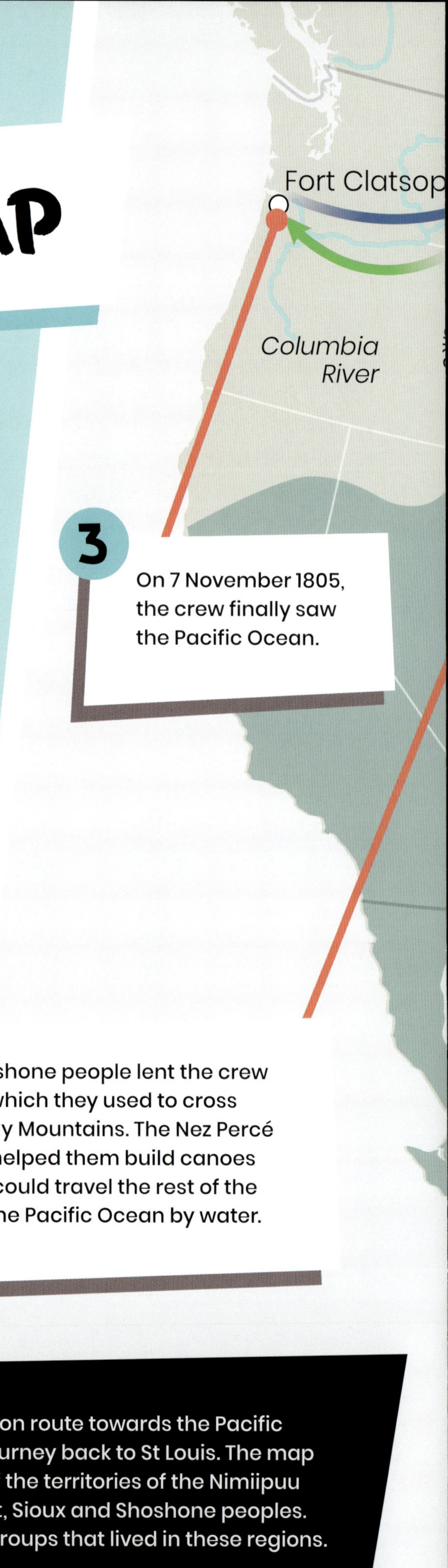

**3**

On 7 November 1805, the crew finally saw the Pacific Ocean.

**2**

The Shoshone people lent the crew horses which they used to cross the Rocky Mountains. The Nez Percé people helped them build canoes so they could travel the rest of the way to the Pacific Ocean by water.

The green arrows show the expedition route towards the Pacific Ocean. The blue arrows show the journey back to St Louis. The map has markers to show the location of the territories of the Nimiipuu (also known as Nez Percé), Blackfeet, Sioux and Shoshone peoples. These are some of the Indigenous groups that lived in these regions.

4

While the Corps of Discovery all took the same route to the Pacific Ocean, they split up on their way home. They hoped this would allow them to explore a larger area of land. In July 1806, Lewis and a group of men travelled north to explore the Marias River and the northern edge of the land gained through the Louisiana Purchase. Clark took another group south to explore the Yellowstone River.

5

The group came back together at Fort Mandan, where they had spent the winter of 1804 to 1805, then continued the rest of the way home together.

6

The Corps of Discovery finally returned home on 23 September 1806.

1

Lewis, Clark and their crew began their journey up the Missouri River in a **keelboat**. However, as their trip progressed, they used different modes of transportation with the help of Indigenous groups.

# A Land of Many Cultures

Lewis and Clark's **voyage** took them through vast areas of undeveloped land. This was possible thanks to the Louisiana Purchase – a huge area of land that France sold to the United States. France needed the money for their military. For his part, President Jefferson saw it as a way to make the United States richer. It would also make the country bigger and more important on the world stage.

France and the United States signed a **treaty** to make the Louisiana Purchase official in Paris, France, on 2 May 1803. In total, the land cost about $15 million (well over £300 million in today's money). It doubled the size of the United States.

## EXPEDITION ANNOUNCED

President Jefferson announced that Lewis would lead an expedition to explore the new land. But as many as 100,000 people already lived on this land. This included hundreds of communities of Indigenous peoples, as well as enslaved and free Black American people and white **settlers**.

At the time of the expedition, there were over 500 different groups of Indigenous peoples in North America, with as many as 300 languages.

## DIFFERENT CULTURES

Indigenous cultures were very different from American settler cultures. The ways of life of various Indigenous groups also varied from one another. They spoke different languages. Some groups were farmers, growing crops like corn, squash and tobacco. Others led **nomadic** lives – they did not have permanent homes but moved around a lot, following bison herds.

## Think about it

Do you think the land ever really belonged to France or the United States? Or did it belong to the Indigenous peoples? What does this say about attitudes to Indigenous communities at the time?

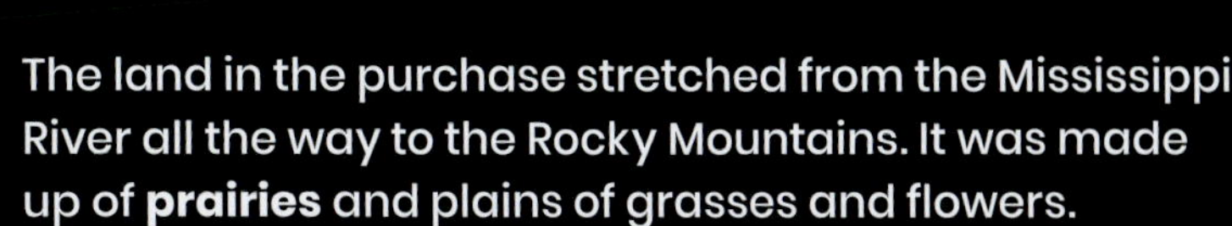

The land in the purchase stretched from the Mississippi River all the way to the Rocky Mountains. It was made up of **prairies** and plains of grasses and flowers.

## CLAIMS ON THE LAND

Some Indigenous communities moved across the land without having a permanent home. But Europeans believed in land ownership. And the US was eager to claim the land they had bought. This was one of the main goals of the Lewis and Clark expedition. Eventually, the US forced many Indigenous communities off the land they had called home for centuries.

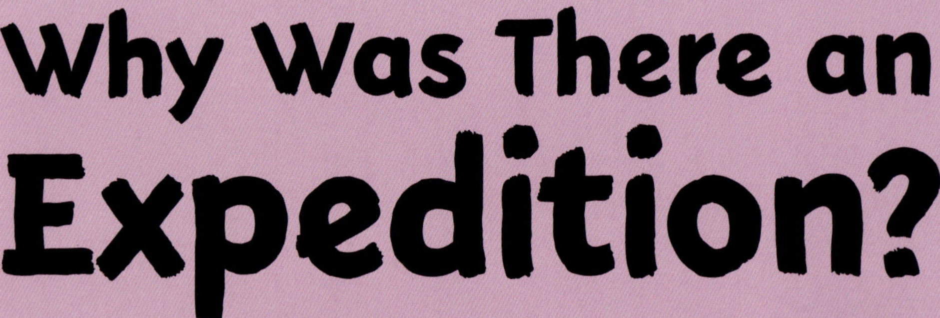

# Why Was There an Expedition?

On 18 January 1803, President Jefferson sent a secret request to Congress. In it, he asked for $2,500 (about £56,000 in today's money) to pay for an expedition along the Missouri River. He had many reasons for his request. He wanted to expand trade and improve scientific knowledge. He also wanted to develop relationships with Indigenous communities. Finally, he wanted to strengthen the United States' claim over the land.

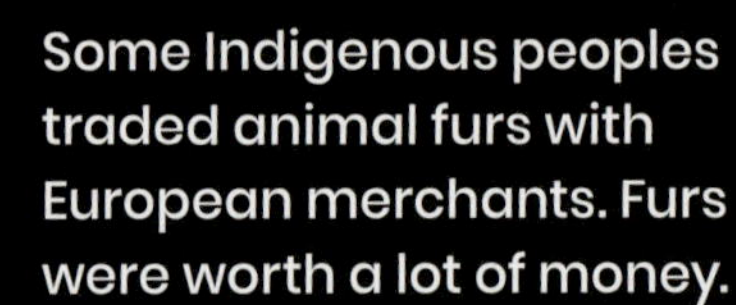

Some Indigenous peoples traded animal furs with European merchants. Furs were worth a lot of money.

## EXPANDING TRADE

President Jefferson wanted to learn more about the land. One of his goals was to find the **legendary** Northwest Passage. He had been fascinated by this route since he was a child. If found, the passage would allow people to travel by boat from the Atlantic Ocean to the Pacific Ocean. This would help expand trade for the United States.

The Northwest Passage was not discovered until 1851, long after the end of the expedition. This map, which covers the area around the Arctic Circle, is from 1772. It shows the different routes taken by some famous explorers, such as Bartholomew de Fonte, in search of the Northwest Passage.

## RELATIONSHIPS WITH INDIGENOUS PEOPLES

President Jefferson wanted to improve the American economy. He also hoped to create better relationships with Indigenous peoples. He thought doing so would encourage them to give up their nomadic lifestyles and take up farming. For President Jefferson, this was all part of his plan to get more land. He thought if Indigenous people were farmers, they would be more likely to sell their land to the United States.

## Think about it

Why would a water route from the east coast to the west coast have benefited trade for the United States?

## STAKING A CLAIM

The United States hoped to gain an understanding of the land's resources, people and **geography**. This would help the country make use of its new purchase. It would also help stake a claim to the land. President Jefferson hoped that, eventually, the United States would stretch across the continent. It would have power and influence around the world.

## SCIENTIFIC CURIOSITY

President Jefferson had a lot of scientific **curiosity**. He wondered what living things the expedition crew would find. For example, he was fascinated by mastodons. These massive animals were similar to woolly mammoths. President Jefferson wanted to see if the explorers would find any living examples. Once the Louisiana Purchase was public knowledge, people were curious about this too.

Many of the crew members drew plants and animals they saw on their journey. This bird, called a sage grouse, was drawn by Clark on the expedition.

# Getting Ready

President Jefferson chose Lewis to lead the expedition. Lewis was President Jefferson's personal secretary. They had known each other since Lewis was a child. Lewis asked Clark to lead the expedition with him. Clark was not recognised as an equal partner by the US government, but Lewis considered him as such. Lewis and Clark gathered a crew of around 45 men to join them. They called their group the Corps of Discovery. Lewis also brought Seaman, a large, docile Newfoundland dog, on the trip.

Lewis wrote this list in 1803. It shows the many gifts he bought to give to Indigenous peoples during the trip.

Lewis and Clark had served together in the army. This had given them experience with Indigenous groups and the **frontier**. This engraving is from the 19th century. It shows Lewis and Clark trying to make friends with Indigenous people.

This photo from the Lewis and Clark National Historic Trail Interpretive Center shows a model of what the crew's boats would have looked like.

## PREPARING FOR THE TRIP

Before the group set out, President Jefferson sent Lewis to Philadelphia, Pennsylvania, to prepare. There, Lewis spent time studying natural history. He studied medicine, **astronomy**, **zoology** and **botany**. He also learned to **navigate** using the stars. Lewis looked through maps and journals. He wanted to learn as much as possible about the mostly unmapped area. He also bought a lot of gifts to give Indigenous peoples, such as beads, ribbons and mirrors.

The crew brought along many supplies for the long journey. This included navigation and mapmaking tools, **compasses**, food, clothing, medical supplies, books, maps, camping supplies and weapons. They also had boats built to help them travel.

## Fascinating fact

Historians estimate that Lewis and Clark took more than 27 metric tons (30 tons) of supplies with them on their trip. That is about the same weight as five large elephants!

This image shows just a few of the tools that would have been taken on the expedition, including a telescope, an axe and a compass. Lewis's packing list had hundreds of items on it.

# Heading West

The crew members of the Corps of Discovery left from Camp Dubois (also known as Camp Wood) near St Louis, Missouri, on 14 May 1804. They travelled in a large boat and two smaller boats, heading west along the Missouri River. The crew included hunters, blacksmiths and carpenters. Most were soldiers or volunteers. One member, York, was an enslaved Black man. He had been enslaved by Clark's family and was forced to join Clark on the journey.

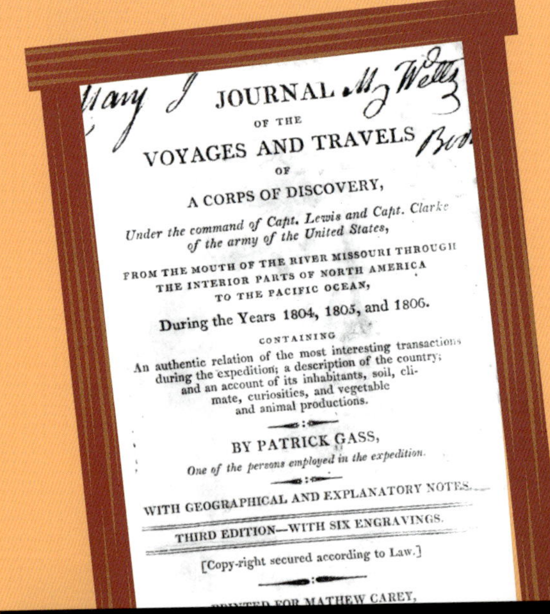

JOURNAL

OF THE

VOYAGES AND TRAVELS

OF

A CORPS OF DISCOVERY,

*Under the command of Capt. Lewis and Capt. Clarke of the army of the United States,*

FROM THE MOUTH OF THE RIVER MISSOURI THROUGH THE INTERIOR PARTS OF NORTH AMERICA TO THE PACIFIC OCEAN,

During the Years 1804, 1805, and 1806.

CONTAINING

An authentic relation of the most interesting transactions during the expedition; a description of the country; and an account of its inhabitants, soil, climate, curiosities, and vegetable and animal productions.

BY PATRICK GASS,

*One of the persons employed in the expedition.*

WITH GEOGRAPHICAL AND EXPLANATORY NOTES.

THIRD EDITION—WITH SIX ENGRAVINGS.

[Copy-right secured according to Law.]

FOR MATHEW CAREY,

As they set out, crew member Patrick Gass wrote about feeling confident and nervous at the same time. He published his journals from the expedition in 1807.

## INDEPENDENCE DAY ON THE EXPEDITION

On 4 July 1804, the crew camped in an area that Clark described in his journal as one of the most beautiful plains he had ever seen. They named this place Independence Creek to **commemorate** the holiday. This land belonged to the Kanza people. But their village was empty. Lewis and Clark assumed it had been **abandoned**. They were mistaken. The Kanza people were away hunting bison.

The Kanza people are known today as the Kaw Nation. They live in what is now Oklahoma and Kansas. This painting from 1822 shows White Plume, the Kanza chief at that time. It gives an idea of Kanza culture in the early 1800s.

This engraving shows Lewis and Clark meeting with some of the Oto people. It was made by Gass on the expedition.

## FIRST ENCOUNTERS WITH INDIGENOUS COMMUNITIES

Lewis and Clark held a meeting with members of the Missouri and Oto peoples on 3 August 1804. This was their first meeting with Indigenous groups. They named the place where they met Council Bluff. This area is near present-day Council Bluffs, Iowa. That month, they also held a meeting with the Yankton Sioux people in what is now Yankton, South Dakota.

## AN UNFORTUNATE DEATH

Along the way, the crew faced many challenges. This included **dysentery**, tick bites and other **ailments**. The youngest member of the group, Charles Floyd, died on 20 August 1804. He was 22 years old. It is believed he suffered a ruptured **appendix** while the group were in what is now Iowa.

## Fascinating fact

Members of the crew were given special roles based on their skills. This included a blacksmith for repairs, hunters to catch food and a medic to treat the sick and injured.

*Floyd's Grave*, an 1832 painting, shows the hilltop where Lewis and Clark buried Sergeant Floyd.

# Fort Mandan

In late October 1804, the crew reached the villages of the Mandan and Hidatsa peoples. This was near what is now the city of Bismarck, North Dakota. The crew decided to stay here for the winter. While they were with the Mandan people, the crew witnessed many **rituals**. In one, the Mandan people offered food to a **sacred** buffalo skull. They hoped this would bring them more buffalo to hunt.

### MEETING SACAGAWEA

Around this time, the group took on a French-Canadian fur trader named Toussaint Charbonneau. Charbonneau acted as an interpreter for the group as they travelled to the Pacific Ocean. They needed him to help them speak with the Shoshone people, who they hoped would give them horses to ride across the Rocky Mountains. Sacagawea, Charbonneau's wife, joined them as well. She was a young Shoshone woman who had been kidnapped by the Hidatsa people at the age of 12. Charbonneau had then paid for her to be his wife.

In the autumn of 1804, Sacagawea was 16 years old and pregnant. Her son was born during the expedition, on 11 February 1805. He was named was Jean Baptiste. This sculpture in Bismarck shows mother and son together.

The crew spent four weeks building a triangular-shaped fort with pointed stakes all around it. They named it Fort Mandan as a tribute to the Mandan people. This photo shows a modern reconstruction of the fort. The original site is now underwater.

## Fascinating fact

Changes in the course of the Missouri River and nearby dam projects mean the original site of Fort Mandan is almost certainly underwater and evidence of where it was originally built may never be found.

This is one of the many maps drawn by Clark on the expedition. It shows areas around the Columbia River, which separates Oregon and Washington.

### WINTER ACTIVITIES

The crew spent five months at Fort Mandan. They hunted, **foraged** and made clothing and canoes. Lewis and Clark organised information and samples from the start of their expedition. This included maps, minerals, plant specimens, animals, artefacts, reports and letters. Live animals, including a prairie dog and magpies, were sent back to President Jefferson.

# From Mandan to the Pacific

On 7 April 1805, a small group left the expedition. They had the important task of taking some of the prepared plant and animal samples, maps and papers to President Jefferson. Meanwhile, the rest of the crew left Fort Mandan and continued their journey towards the Pacific Ocean. The expedition crew was now down to 33 people.

### CHANGING LUCK

Lewis and Clark soon realised that the water passage to the Pacific Ocean that President Jefferson hoped to find did not exist. Around this time, they met the Salish people. At first, the Salish people had debated whether to kill the crew, but eventually decided to show them hospitality. Lewis wrote in his journal about the harsh conditions of the mountains. Luckily, in August the crew met a group of Shoshone people. Sacagawea's brother Cameahwait was their chief. Sacagawea helped the crew to communicate with the Shoshone people by providing translations.

## Think about it

Why do you think Sacagawea was an important member of the expedition?

This illustration shows Sacagawea leading the crew from Fort Mandan west to the Rocky Mountains. It was drawn by Alfred Russell in 1904.

## A DIFFICULT JOURNEY

The Shoshone people gave the crew horses and a guide. This helped them cross the Bitterroot Range, which is part of the Rocky Mountains. This was the most difficult part of the trip. At one point, the crew got lost. Although they crossed in September, they dealt with extreme temperatures that led to **frostbite**. They were hungry, thirsty and tired.

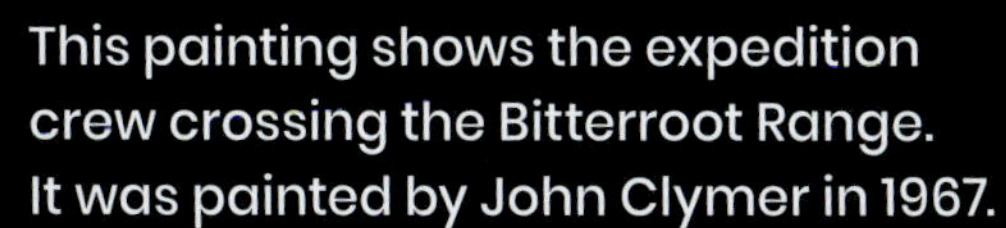

This painting shows the expedition crew crossing the Bitterroot Range. It was painted by John Clymer in 1967.

## THE PACIFIC OCEAN

The Nez Percé people helped the crew recover after their difficult **trek** over the mountains and kept the crew's horses for them. They also helped them build canoes. This would allow the crew to keep travelling by water. On 7 November 1805, the crew got their first view of the Pacific Ocean. And in mid-November, they finally reached it. This was 18 months after they had set off from Missouri.

Lewis and Clark finally reached the Pacific Ocean near what is now the town of Seaside, Oregon. A statue of Lewis and Clark stands at the end of the promenade to mark the furthest point in their expedition, before they began the long journey home.

# Finally Reunited

**Meriwether Lewis**
One of the leaders of the expedition

**William Clark**
The other leader of the expedition

**York**
An enslaved man and Clark's servant

**Sacagawea**
A Shoshone woman living with the Hidatsa people

**Toussaint Charbonneau**
Sacagawea's husband, also living in the Hidatsa village

**Jean Baptiste Charbonneau**
Sacagawea and Charbonneau's son

**Cameahwait**
Sacagawea's brother and a Shoshone chief

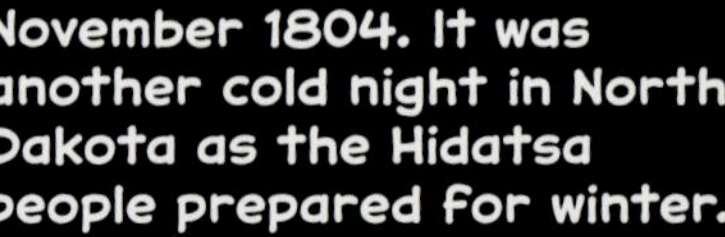


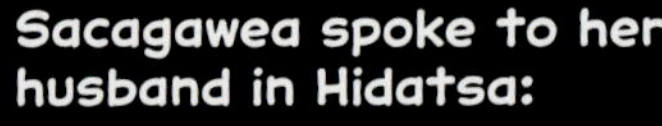

Lewis, Clark and their crew spent the winter of 1804-1805 at Fort Mandan, near Hidatsa Village.

When spring arrived, the group set off westwards.

Sacagawea spoke to her son in Hidatsa:
We are going to travel far and wide. Are you excited, little one?

Brace, everyone!

All of Lewis's maps and papers fell out the boat into the river.

Thank you! We could not do this without you!

August 1805, Montana.
How long can we last, Clark?

We can last a few days.

The crew met a group of Shoshone people.
Perhaps we should go and speak to them.

But we can't speak their language.

Sacagawea and Charbonneau spoke both Hidatsa and Shoshoni.
Sacagawea speaks their language. She could translate for us.

These are my people – I'm sure they will help us.

Sacagawea spoke to the Shoshone people in their language:
We are tired, and we need a place to rest.

Suddenly, a man burst through the crowd and called out in Shoshoni:
Sister!

Cameahwait!

Cameahwait was Sacagawea's brother, but they had not seen each other in years.

I've got someone I need to introduce to you.

His name is Jean Baptiste.

# A Challenging Winter

This entry in Clark's journal from 24 November 1805 lists the votes from the crew on where to stay. It includes York's name.

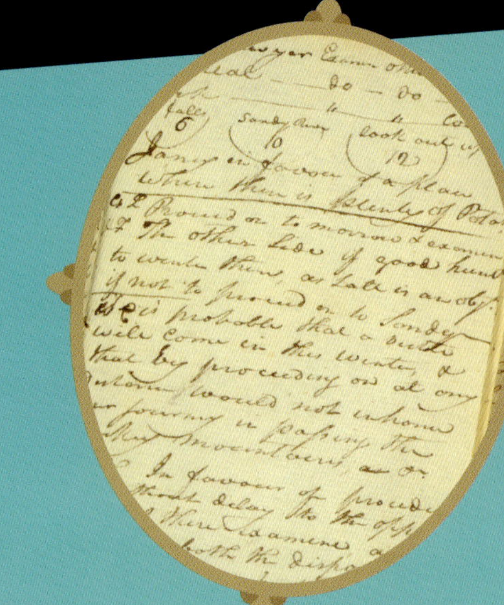

By November 1805, the expedition group had accomplished their main goals and were ready to go home. They hoped to find ships along the Pacific Coast to take them, but were unable to. With winter fast approaching, they needed to find a place to stay until the spring. Lewis and Clark asked their crew to vote on where they should stay for the next five months. The crew chose to camp south of the Columbia River, near what is now Astoria, Oregon. It is here that they built Fort Clatsop.

## Think about it

York was included in the vote to decide where to stay, even though Black men were not allowed to vote in the United States at this time. Several years later, York asked for his freedom. Clark said no. What does this say about York's value in the expedition and Clark's view of him?

Today, you can visit a reconstruction of Fort Clatsop.

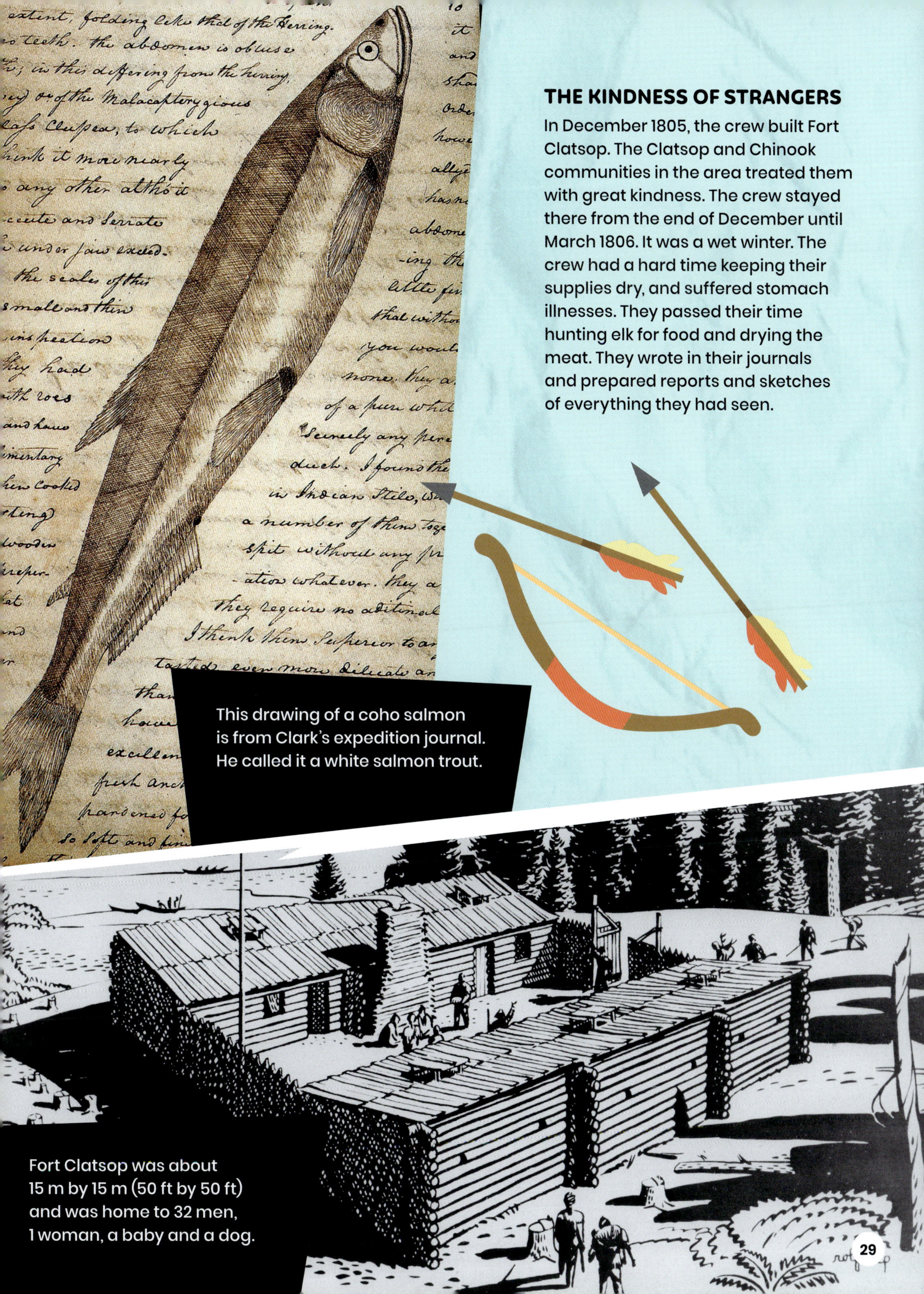

## THE KINDNESS OF STRANGERS

In December 1805, the crew built Fort Clatsop. The Clatsop and Chinook communities in the area treated them with great kindness. The crew stayed there from the end of December until March 1806. It was a wet winter. The crew had a hard time keeping their supplies dry, and suffered stomach illnesses. They passed their time hunting elk for food and drying the meat. They wrote in their journals and prepared reports and sketches of everything they had seen.

This drawing of a coho salmon is from Clark's expedition journal. He called it a white salmon trout.

Fort Clatsop was about 15 m by 15 m (50 ft by 50 ft) and was home to 32 men, 1 woman, a baby and a dog.

# Returning Home

The Columbia River could be very dangerous. This painting by Charles Marion Russell is from 1905. It shows the expedition crew travelling in canoes on the river.

In March 1806, the crew began the long journey home. They stole a canoe from members of the Clatsop people. They sailed up the Columbia River, going back the way they had came. When they reached the Nez Percé community, they retrieved their horses and waited for the winter snows to melt so they could continue their journey home. Lewis wrote about the Clatsop people setting fir trees on fire as they believed it was a way to ensure good weather for the journey ahead.

Clark carved his name on a large rock formation. He called it Pompey's Pillar. This was after Sacagawea's son Jean Baptiste, whom he called Pomp.

## SPLITTING UP

The crew split up into four smaller groups on their way home. This was so they could explore more land on the way back. They agreed to meet up at Fort Mandan. While they were apart, the horses of Clark's group were stolen. This was believed to have been done by members of the Crow community.

The killing of the Blackfeet individuals was the first and only deadly conflict of the expedition. This historic sign marks the area where the conflict happened.

## A DEADLY CONFLICT

Meanwhile, Lewis's dog Seaman was stolen by members of the Watlala community. Their chief said he did not approve of the theft. Months later, Lewis and his group travelled to an area where they were seen as a threat. There, some Blackfeet people tried to steal their weapons and horses. A fight broke out and two of the Blackfeet people were killed. Lewis and his men got away on their horses and rode non-stop for 24 hours to escape.

This statue of Lewis, Clark and Seaman is in St Louis, Missouri. This is where their expedition started and ended.

## ARRIVING HOME

The four groups met up at Fort Mandan, from where Sacagawea and her family left to return home. All the remaining members of the expedition crew arrived in St Louis on 23 September 1806. People celebrated their arrival. Their expedition had taken two years, four months and nine days. They had travelled close to 13,000 km (8,000 miles) on their journey.

## Think about it

Many people assumed the expedition crew had died on their journey. Why might they have thought this?

# Westward Expansion

The Lewis and Clark expedition had a major impact on scientific knowledge and US society. The crew recorded more than 120 animal species and 200 plant species. They had peaceful interactions with several Indigenous groups. President Jefferson used this information as well as the maps they made to make plans for the land he had purchased from France.

This painting shows the idea of **manifest destiny** as a woman. She is leading American settlers and railroads west. Indigenous people are running from her. It was painted in 1872 by John Gast.

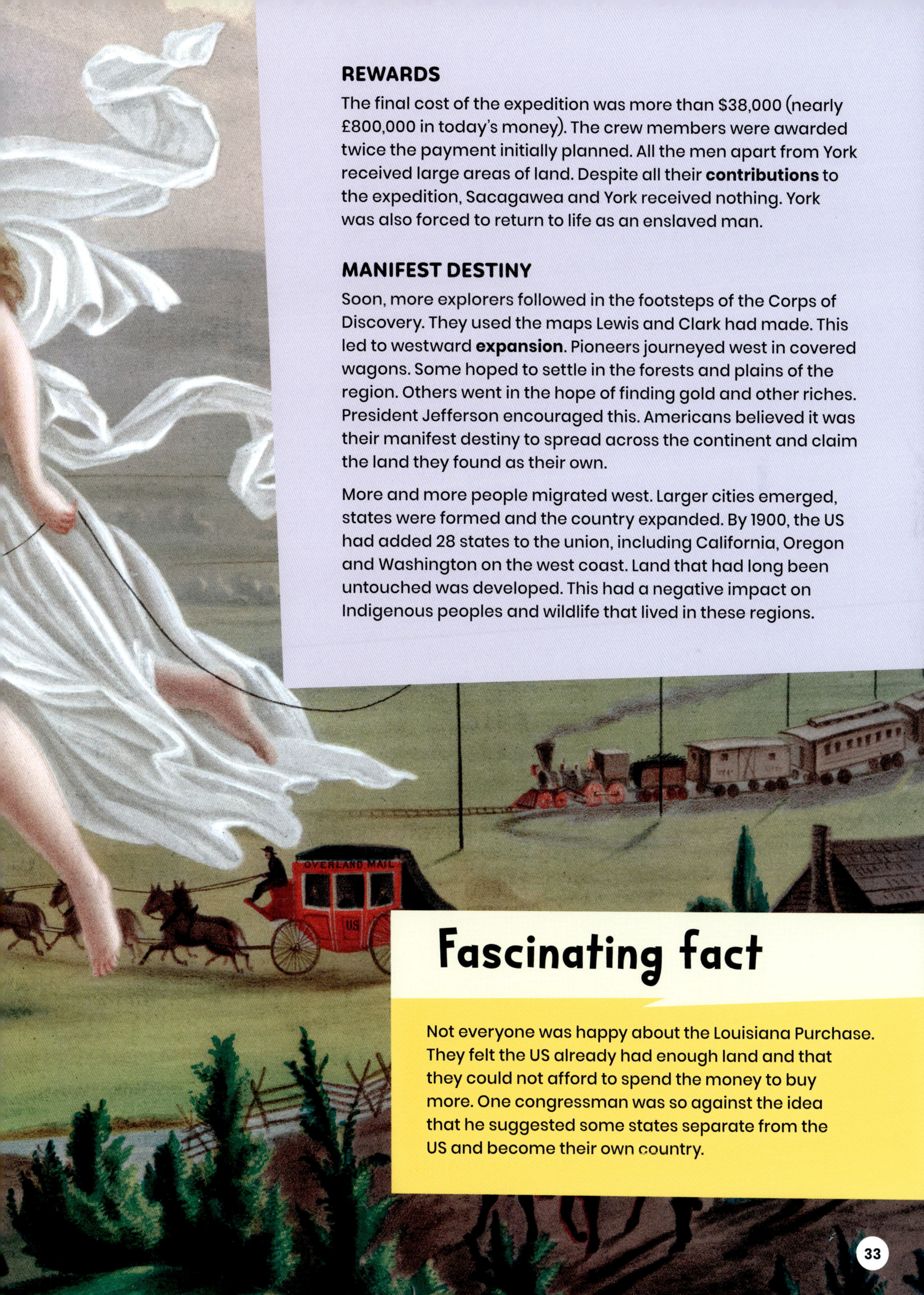


### REWARDS

The final cost of the expedition was more than $38,000 (nearly £800,000 in today's money). The crew members were awarded twice the payment initially planned. All the men apart from York received large areas of land. Despite all their **contributions** to the expedition, Sacagawea and York received nothing. York was also forced to return to life as an enslaved man.

### MANIFEST DESTINY

Soon, more explorers followed in the footsteps of the Corps of Discovery. They used the maps Lewis and Clark had made. This led to westward **expansion**. Pioneers journeyed west in covered wagons. Some hoped to settle in the forests and plains of the region. Others went in the hope of finding gold and other riches. President Jefferson encouraged this. Americans believed it was their manifest destiny to spread across the continent and claim the land they found as their own.

More and more people migrated west. Larger cities emerged, states were formed and the country expanded. By 1900, the US had added 28 states to the union, including California, Oregon and Washington on the west coast. Land that had long been untouched was developed. This had a negative impact on Indigenous peoples and wildlife that lived in these regions.

## Fascinating fact

Not everyone was happy about the Louisiana Purchase. They felt the US already had enough land and that they could not afford to spend the money to buy more. One congressman was so against the idea that he suggested some states separate from the US and become their own country.

# Indigenous People's Perspectives

The Lewis and Clark expedition was a huge success in the opinions of the US government and many of its citizens. So was the westward expansion of American settlers. However, it had a devastating effect on the Indigenous communities who had lived on the land for thousands of years.

## INDIAN REMOVAL ACT

Most interactions between the expedition crew and Indigenous peoples had been peaceful and friendly. Despite that, Congress passed the Indian Removal Act in 1830. As a direct result of the act, entire Indigenous communities were forcibly removed from their land. Some of them tried to fight to keep their land, but were met with US military force. The removal of Indigenous peoples was intended to be done in a **humane** way, but thousands of them were killed.

About 60,000 Indigenous people were forced to walk from their homes in the southeastern US to land west of the Mississippi River. The journey was 1,600 km (1,000 miles). As many as 16,000 people died. This is known as the Trail of Tears.

## CULTURAL ERASURE

Americans thought it was their destiny to spread across the land. They also thought it was their right and responsibility to spread American culture. Indigenous peoples who wanted to stay on their land were expected to adopt an American way of life. In the 1870s, Indigenous children were forced to live far away from their families at dedicated boarding schools. They were forced to change their names and cut their hair. They endured many types of mistreatment and some children even died at these schools.

The US government wanted to **assimilate** Indigenous communities. This meant making them give up their language and culture to fit in with the American way of life. Deb Haaland, an American politician, said "This was a concerted attempt to **eradicate** the quote, 'Indian problem' — to either assimilate or destroy Native peoples altogether" (*The Independent*, 2024).

Deb Haaland is an American politician from New Mexico and a member of the Pueblo Laguna Indigenous community. Haaland's grandparents were forced to attend a boarding school.

## Think about it

On 25 October 2024, President Joe Biden apologised for the US government's role in creating boarding schools where Indigenous youth were forcibly sent. Why do you think it has taken so long since the event for the government to apologise?

This photo was taken around 1890. It shows Indigenous children at a boarding school. Their hair is closely cut. They are wearing typical American dress of the time.

# Lessons from History

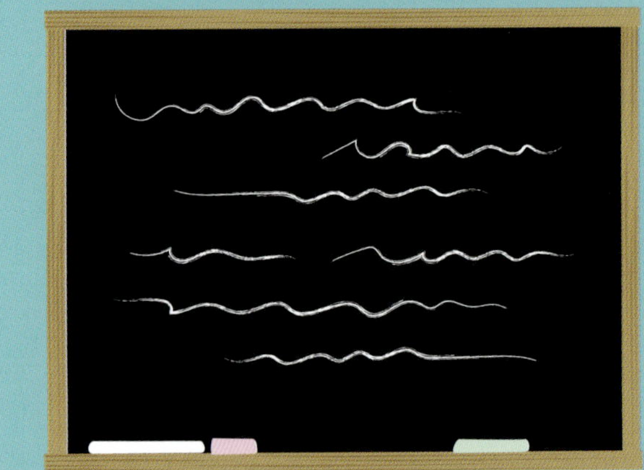

Throughout history, many people have travelled through the land that is now the United States. So why do we remember the Lewis and Clark expedition, and what can we learn from it?

## CONTRIBUTIONS OF THE EXPEDITION

The Lewis and Clark expedition was the first time Americans had formally travelled west of the Mississippi River to explore the land. The group discovered new plants and animals and they met people that American citizens had never seen or even heard of before. All the knowledge they gathered and recorded greatly informed the geographical knowledge of North America. Their findings helped to expand trade and fuel curiosity about nature and different cultures.

The National Museum of the American Indian is in Washington, DC. It was established in 1989 and is devoted to preserving Indigenous cultures and histories.

## RIGHTS OF INDIGENOUS PEOPLES

France sold land that people already lived on to the United States. The United States then forced these people off that land. This illustrates what society was like at the time. The fact that children were taken from their families and stripped of their **heritage** further paints this picture.

The US government and American settlers used religion to justify their actions. They said they were destined by God to spread across the continent. They claimed they were doing what was best for the Indigenous peoples. But if Americans were really acting in the interests of Indigenous communities, they would have allowed them to make decisions for themselves instead.

### Think about it

The expedition crew were all men, except for Sacagawea. Sacagawea was kidnapped as a child. She was then sold to Charbonneau to be his wife when she was just a teenager. What does this suggest about attitudes to women at the time?

This statue of York was created by Ed Hamilton in 2003. It is in Louisville, Kentucky.

## RIGHTS OF BLACK AMERICAN PEOPLE

York was not given the choice to make his own decisions when he was forced to accompany Clark. York was smart and skilled enough to contribute to the expedition. His opinion was important enough that he was able to vote on where the crew would stay for the winter. Yet, when York asked Clark for his freedom, Clark refused. This shows Clark's view of York and highlights the injustices faced by enslaved Black American people at this time.

## Uncovering the Truth

# Primary Sources

A lot is known about the people and events of this famed expedition. This is because there are so many primary sources still available to historians today. A primary source is a document or object created at the time of a historical event.

### Primary sources include

- official documents
- letters
- diaries
- paintings or drawings
- photographs
- sound recordings
- videos

Photo of original source

### DIFFERENT POINTS OF VIEW

Primary and secondary sources may tell different stories depending on the views of the people who created them. A member of the expedition would have a different perspective from an Indigenous person who was forced off their land. It is important to question sources – doing this helps us to understand them and understand different perspectives better.

### SECRET LETTER

This is a secret letter that was sent by President Jefferson to Congress. In it, he asked for $2,500 to fund the expedition. He wrote it on 18 January 1803, before the start of the expedition. It explains why the expedition should take place and asks Congress for money to pay for it.

Original source text

The appropriation of two thousand five hundred dollars, "for the purpose of extending the external commerce of the US", while understood and considered by the Executive as giving the legislative sanction, would cover the undertaking from notice, and prevent the obstructions which interested individuals might otherwise previously prepare in its way.

The $2,500 set aside "to expand the United States' trade with other countries" is understood as giving Congress's approval for the expedition. This will keep the project under the radar and prevent anyone with a personal interest from interfering.

Look at the letter, then read the transcribed version of the text and answer the questions below.

## Quick questions

- Why did President Jefferson not want Congress to say they were funding the expedition?
- This letter is over 200 years old. Many letters of that time have been lost or destroyed. Why has this been preserved?
- One dollar in 1803 would be worth nearly $28 (about £22) today. Can you work out how much President Jefferson asked Congress for in today's money?

## Discussion questions

- Who may have opposed the idea of the expedition?
- Why did President Jefferson think that the expedition would improve trade with other countries?
- Is there anything about the expedition that you think President Jefferson may not have included?

- So that people could not interfere and stop it from happening.
- It has been preserved as an important primary source written by President Jefferson.
- About $70,000 (about £56,000).

# Uncovering the Truth

# Secondary Sources

A secondary source is a document or object created after the event, or by someone who was not directly involved in the event. Secondary sources can explain or interpret primary sources. They help in understanding an event.

### Secondary sources include

- news articles
- books
- media documentaries
- encyclopaedias

## A MYSTERIOUS STATUE

On 20 February 2021, someone erected a statue of York in Mount Tabor Park in the city of Portland, Oregon. The Lewis and Clark expedition crew had camped near the site of the present-day city in 1806. The statue shows York's face with his name written below. It also includes a detailed description of how York contributed to the expedition.

The statue was created by an artist who was initially **anonymous**. The bust was made of wood and a plastic-like material rather than metal or stone. It is thought this was because it was only intended to be temporary. It was later damaged and is not currently on display.

A statue of York was installed in Portland.

Original source text

York

The first African American to cross North America and reach the Pacific Coast.

Born into slavery in the 1770s to the family of William Clark, York became a member of the 1804 Lewis and Clark Expedition. Though York was an enslaved laborer, he performed all the duties of a full member of the expedition. He was a skilled hunter, negotiated trade with Native American communities, and tended to the sick. Upon his return east with the Corps of Discovery, York asked for his freedom. Clark refused his request.

The date and circumstances of his death are unclear.

The sculptor who made this statue eventually revealed himself as local artist Todd McGrain. He wanted York's contributions to the Lewis and Clark expedition to be celebrated. He also wanted to make people think about how little York was valued and the injustices he faced.

Many people visited the statue and left tributes such as flowers. However, the statue was also knocked over and attacked. This shows that not everyone agreed with the sculptor's message and that racism remains a problem today.

Look at the statue, then read the transcribed version of the text and answer the questions below.

## Quick questions

- What materials were used to create the statue?
- What were some of York's tasks?
- What is the purpose of this statue?

## Discussion questions

- What might have motivated the artist to put up this statue?
- Why do you think the artist chose materials that would not last?
- Why do you think we know the first names of other people in the expedition, but not York's?

- Wood and a plastic-like material.
- Hunting, negotiating trade agreements and looking after sick people.
- To demonstrate that York was just as important as the other members of the Corps of Discovery, and to show the injustices he faced.

# Vocabulary Builder
# Exploring the Land

What might a journal entry from the Lewis and Clark expedition look like? Read this fictional journal entry to see what information one of the crew might have included. Pay attention to key words that describe the expedition.

28 July 1804

We set off on our expedition two months ago to explore the great lands of our country.

We are aiming to satisfy the president's goals and serve our nation. The president believes expansion is our destiny. He will stop at nothing until we achieve it.

As we make our trek, we are recording the geography, resources, and plant and animal specimens we find. We are travelling by waterway. We hope to soon reach the coast of the Pacific Ocean. We are trading with the Indigenous peoples, who generously share their knowledge of the land with us. They are also helping us navigate our route. It has been an exciting voyage so far, and I can't wait to see who we meet and what we discover next.

**Imagine you are keeping a record of a trip to explore a place that is new to you. Then use the journal entry on page 42 and the prompts and word bank below to write your own entry.**

- **What do you see?**
- **Who do you meet?**
- **How do you feel?**

| | |
|---|---|
| **Landscape** | coast, environment, forests, geography, mountains, oceans, plains, rivers, animals, plants, surroundings, wildlife |
| **Motivations** | culture, curiosity, discover, experiences, foods, explore, learn, languages, meet people, sightsee |
| **Travelling** | boat, expedition, hike, journey, navigate, route, sail, trek, voyage, walk |

# Glossary

**Abandoned** To be left for good or deserted.

**Ailment** A sickness, disease or injury.

**Appendix** An organ in the human body. It can burst and cause great sickness or even death.

**Apprehensive** To feel uncertainty or dread.

**Assimilate** To absorb one culture into another.

**Astronomy** The study of the universe, including the planets and stars.

**Botany** The study of plants.

**Captain** A rank in the military. A captain commands other soldiers.

**Carpenter** A person who builds things using wood, such as furniture or houses.

**Commemorate** To memorialise or otherwise remember something historic.

**Compass** A handheld tool that shows the four cardinal directions — north, east, south and west.

**Contribution** An important action that makes a difference, or something, such as money, that is given to help.

**Culture** The way of life of a group of people, including their language, clothes, celebrations and art.

**Curiosity** To have an interest in the unknown.

**Declaration of Independence** The document that marked the independence of the American colonies from Great Britain and the founding of the United States.

**Dysentery** An illness that causes major stomach upset and even death. It is often caused by drinking unclean water.

**Enslaved** To be forced to work for someone else without the freedom to stop or leave.

**Eradicate** To get rid of or erase.

**Expansion** The act of growing or spreading out.

**Expedition** A trip or journey that is done for a reason, or with a particular goal in mind.

**Foraged** To search for food in the wild.

**Frontier** An area of land that is beyond what a society considers as settled.

**Frostbite** An injury to the skin caused by extremely cold temperatures.

**Geography** The features of an area of land.

**Government** A group of people who have been given the power to make and enforce laws in a specific area. Everyone who lives in the area must obey these laws.

**Heritage** Parts of the culture of a community, including their art, language and customs, which have come from the past generations and are still important.

**Historic** The first of its kind, or important enough to be remembered for a long time.

**Humane** To be considerate, kind or sympathetic towards humans and other living things.

**Indigenous** Indigenous peoples are groups of people who are the original inhabitants of a region or area. There may be many different groups of Indigenous peoples within a region, each with their own languages and cultures.

**Interpreter** Someone who translates oral speech, so that people speaking different languages can communicate with one another.

**Keelboat** A long, narrow boat with a flat keel (base).

**Legendary** To be famous, with many stories told about it. Something legendary may not always be true.

**Lieutenant** A rank in the military. A lieutenant is below a captain.

**Manifest destiny** The belief held by Americans in the 19th century that it was their God-given right to expand westwards.

**Navigate** To travel or find one's way.

**Nomadic** To move from place to place.

**Prairie** A wide expanse of temperate grassland with few trees. Prairies are found in North America.

**Resource** Something that people and other living things want or need.

**Ritual** An action that is carried out in a specific way. Rituals are often part of religious or spiritual practice.

**Route** A path that can be travelled.

**Sacred** To be holy, or of great spiritual importance.

**Sergeant** A rank in the military. A sergeant is below a lieutenant.

**Settlers** A group of people who move away from one area to live in a new one.

**Source** A written document, artefact or building that provides information relating to the past. Sources are also known as evidence.

**Species** A group of living things that have similar features and can produce young.

**Specimen** A sample. It is often of plants, animals or natural material that may contain living things, such as soil.

**Trade** The exchange of goods between people, groups or countries.

**Treaty** An official agreement between two or more groups, such as two countries. It states how they will act or what they will do.

**Trek** A long journey that can be difficult.

**Voyage** A journey, often by water.

**Wary** To be cautious of or unsure about something.

**Waterway** A body of water, such as a river, that can be travelled through.

**Zoology** The study of animals.

# Index


**B**

Biden, President Joe 35
Bitterroot Range 23
Black American people 12, 28, 37
Blackfeet people 10, 31
boarding schools 35

**C**

Cameahwait 22, 24–27
Camp Dubois 6, 18
canoes 23, 30
Charbonneau, Jean Baptiste 9, 20, 24–27, 30
Charbonneau, Toussaint 7, 9, 20, 24–27
Chinook people 29
claiming land 14–15
Clark, William 4, 8, 15, 16
Clatsop people 29, 30
coho salmon 29
Columbia River 21, 30
contributions 36
Corps of Discovery 4–5, 10, 16, 19, 22
cost of the expedition 33
Council Bluff 19
Crow people 30
cultures 12–13, 35

**D, E**

dangers 19, 23, 29
enslaved people 7, 9, 12, 18, 37
expansion 32–33

**F**

Floyd, Charles 9, 19
Fonte, Bartholomew de 14
Fort Clatsop 28–29
Fort Mandan 7, 11, 20–21
France 12, 37

**G**

Gass, Patrick 9, 18, 19
Gast, John 32–33
gifts, for Indigenous peoples 16–17

**H**

Haaland, Deb 35
Hamilton, Ed 37
Hidatsa people 20
horses 10, 20, 23, 30, 31

**I**

Independence Day 18
Indian Removal Act (1830) 34
Indigenous peoples 4–5, 10–11, 18
- Blackfeet people 10, 31
- Chinook people 29

Indigenous peoples cont.
- Clatsop people 28, 30
- conflict 31
- Crow people 30
- cultures 12–13
- first encounters with the expedition 19
- gifts for 16–17
- Hidatsa people 20
- Indian Removal Act (1830) 34
- Kanza people (Kaw Nation) 18
- kindness of 29
- languages 12–13
- Mandan people 20, 21
- manifest destiny 33
- Missouri people 19
- Nez Percé (Nimiipuu) people 10, 23, 30
- Oto people 19
- perspectives 34–35
- President Jefferson 15
- Pueblo Laguna people 35
- rights 37
- rituals 20
- Salish people 22
- Shoshone people 10, 20, 22–23
- trade 14
- Yankton Sioux people 19

## J

Jefferson, President Thomas 8, 38
- Louisiana Purchase 6, 12
- reasons for the expedition 10, 14–15

## K

Kanza people (Kaw Nation) 18

keelboats 11

## L

languages 12–13

Lewis, Meriwether 4, 8, 16–17, 24–27

Lewis and Clark National Historic Trail Interpretive Center 17

Louisiana Purchase 6, 12–13, 32

## M

magpies 21

Mandan people 20, 21

manifest destiny 32–33

maps
- Columbia River 21
- expedition 10–11
- Louisiana Purchase 6
- Northwest Passage 14
- route 5

Missouri people 19

Marias River 11

Missouri River 21

## N

National Museum of the American Indian 36

Nez Percé (Nimiipuu) people 10, 23, 30

Northwest Passage 14

## O

Ordway, John 9

Oto people 19

## P

Pacific Ocean 7, 22–23

Pompey's Pillar 30

prairie dogs 21

preparing for the trip 16–17

Pueblo Laguna people 35

## R

religion 37

returning home 7, 30–31

rights 37

rituals 20, 30

route 5

## S

Sacagawea 7, 9, 22, 24–27, 33
- arriving home 31
- joining the expedition 20

sage grouse 15

Salish people 22

science 15, 32

Seaman (dog) 9, 16, 31

Seaside (Oregon) 23

Shoshone people 10, 20, 22–23

sources 38–41

statues
- Lewis and Clark 23, 31
- Sacagawea 20
- York 37, 40
- York and Seaman 9

supplies, for the journey 17

## T

trade 4, 14

Trail of Tears 34

## U

United States 32–33, 36–37
- claims on the land 13, 14, 15
- Indigenous communities 34–35
- Louisiana Purchase 11, 12

## W

Watlala people 31

White Plume 18

wildlife 6, 17, 21, 29

winter 7, 11, 21, 25, 28–29

women, attitudes to 37

## Y

Yankton Sioux people 19

Yellowstone River 11

York 9, 18, 24–27, 33, 37–38
- statues 9, 37, 40
- voting 7, 28

# Acknowledgments

The publisher would like to thank the following for their kind permission to reproduce their photographs:

(Key: a-above; b-below/bottom; c-centre; f-far; l-left; r-right; t-top)

**4-5 Alamy Stock Photo**: ClassicStock (t); North Wind Picture Archives (b). **4 Alamy Stock Photo**: IanDagnall Computing (bl). **6 Alamy Stock Photo**: North Wind Picture Archives (bl). **7 Alamy Stock Photo**: Classic Image (br). **Bridgeman Images**: Peter Newark American Pictures (tr). **8 Bridgeman Images**: Royal Geographical Society (bl). **Getty Images**: traveler1116 (cr). **9 Alamy Stock Photo**: History and Art Collection (t); Patti McConville. Sculptor: Bob Scriver (b). **12 Alamy Stock Photo**: IanDagnall Computing (t). **Bridgeman Images**: Peter Newark American Pictures (b). 13 Alamy Stock Photo: John Lambing (b). Bridgeman Images: North Wind Pictures (t). **14 Alamy Stock Photo**: Timewatch Images (t). **Bridgeman Images**: Liszt Collection (b). **15 Alamy Stock Photo**: Granger Historical Picture Archive (b). **Bridgeman Images**: (t). **16 Alamy Stock Photo**: Alpha Stock (tr). **Bridgeman Images**: North Wind Pictures (b). **17 Alamy Stock Photo**: Danita Delimont (b); Witold Skrypczak (t). **18 Getty Images**: MPI (t); Photostock Israel, Science Photo Library (b). **19 Alamy Stock Photo**: Album (b). **Bridgeman Images. 20 Alamy Stock Photo**: Independent Picture Service. **21 Alamy Stock Photo**: Albazil (bl); Don Smetzer (t); Granger Historical Picture Archive (br). **22 Getty Images**: Bettmann (b). **23 Alamy Stock Photo**: Don Denton (bl); Granger Historical Picture Archive (t). **28 Alamy Stock Photo**: Design Pics Inc (b); The Picture Art Collection (t). **29 Alamy Stock Photo**: Granger Historical Picture Archive (tl). **Getty Images**: Kean Collection (b). **30 Alamy Stock Photo**: Danita Delimont (c); Granger Historical Picture Archive (t). **Getty Images**: zrfphoto (b). **31 Alamy Stock Photo**: Jason O. Watson / historical-markers.org (t); Lyroky, Sculptor Harry Weber (br). **32-33 Alamy Stock Photo**: incamerastock. **34 Bridgeman Images**: Look and Learn (b). **35 Alamy Stock Photo**: Everett Collection Historical (b); ZUMA Press, Inc (t). **36 Getty Images**: ULU_BIRD (b). **37 Getty Images**: Douglas Sacha (t). **38 Bridgeman Images**: REUTERS / Molly Riley (b). **40 Getty Images**: Nathan Howard. **43 Getty Images**: Ron and Patty Thomas.

**Cover images:** *Front:* **Alamy Stock Photo:** IanDagnall Computing c; **Dreamstime.com:** Joe Sohm bl; **Getty Images:** Ed Vebell br; Library of Congress, Washington, D.C.: t/ (background); *Back:* **Alamy Stock Photo:** Design Pics Inc b, Granger Historical Picture Archive t, Patti McConville; Sculptor: Bob Scriver c.

**Quote attributions:**

Brown, Matthew. 2024. "Forced assimilation and abuse: How US boarding schools devastated Native American tribes." *The Independent*, October 24.

**Other sources:**

MacGregor, Carol Lynn. 1986. *The Journals of Patrick Gass: Member of the Lewis and Clark Expedition.* Lincoln: University of Nebraska Press, 1986

Lewis, Meriwether, and Clark, William. http://lewisandclarkjournals.unl.edu/

Lewis, Meriwether, Clark, William, and Moulton, Gary E (Ed). 2003. *The Definitive Journals of Lewis and Clark, Vol 9: John Ordway and Charles Floyd.* Winnipeg: Bison Books, 2003

All the books in the DK Super History series have been reviewed by authenticity readers to ensure the represented cultures and experiences are accurate.

This book uses language as appropriate to modern contexts. Historical terms that are no longer acceptable may be present in original source materials and images. These sources are included to present authentic insights into history.